FRINGES

also by Ricardo Quinones

North/South: The Great European Divide
(U Toronto P 2016)

Finishing Touches
(39 West Press 2014)

A Sorting of the Ways: New and Selected Poems
(39 West Press 2011)

Roberta and Other Poems
(39 West Press 2011)

Through the Years
(39 West Press 2010)

Erasmus and Voltaire: Why They Still Matter
(U Toronto P 2010)

Dualisms: The Agons of the Modern World
(U Toronto P 2007)

Foundation Sacrifice in Dante's "Commedia"
(Penn State UP 1994)

The Changes of Cain: Violence and the Lost Brother
(Princeton UP 1991)

Mapping Literary Modernism: Time and Development
(Princeton UP 1985)

Dante Alighieri
(Twayne 1979; updated revised edition 1998)

The Renaissance Discovery of Time
(Harvard UP 1972)

FRINGES

POEMS BY
RICARDO QUINONES

39 WEST
PRESS

39 WEST PRESS
Kansas City, MO
www.39WestPress.com

39 WEST PRESS

Copyright © 2015 by Ricardo Quinones

All rights reserved. No part of this book may be reproduced, scanned, or distributed in any printed or electronic form, including information storage and retrieval systems, without permission. Please do not participate in or encourage piracy of copyrighted materials in violation of the author's rights. Please purchase only authorized editions.

First Edition: September 2015

ISBN: 978-0-9908649-2-9

Library of Congress Control Number: 2015949086

This book is a work of fiction. Names, characters, places, dates, and incidents are products of the author's imagination, or are used fictitiously, satirically, or as parody. Any resemblance to actual persons, living or dead, business establishments, events, or locales is entirely coincidental.

10 9 8 7 6 5 4 3 2

Design, Layout, Front Cover Photo: j.d.tulloch
Back Cover Art Photo: Michele Mattei

39WP-08A

CONTENTS

i.
PROLOGUE: PROGRESS OF THE TIMES

Blinded by Light	3
The Power of Blackness	7
The Crow	10
Missing Nothing	14
Tracking of the Mind	16
Lost and Found	19
The Sneeze: A Holy Terror	21

ii.
EPILOGUE: FOR STEVIE

RETRIEVALS

1. Atonements	27
2. Wanderers	29

i.
PROLOGUE: PROGRESS OF THE TIMES

In lieu of love
Propriety prevailed
Punctuality—a consequence of the Fall—
Made being on time superior far,
Better than having a good time
Justification replaces justice
High principle becomes the rationale
For doing what you ached to do
At which device women excel

State veneer covers all
Men put on vestments of virtue
Cowls of concealment
In whose hot-house hoods
Great schemes germinate
Immense tablets of careful crafting
Written rules of their own drafting
They have entwined themselves
In operations perverse
They are their own captives
Retaliation cranked in reverse.

The great clock tower
Once the locus of civic pride
Becomes a tool of surveillance
A bar to generous affection
A program of neighborly care
Becomes a technique of watcher beware
Vulnerabilities take possession
Guilt is now in session
Fears of exposure, the nasty corners
Where all struggle to survive.
With defenses readily contrived.

Prurience takes root
An infestation infecting all
In their own juices people burn
They repair to the fringes of the city
At the ends of town
Are pleasures found
Enhanced by guilt and dirty down.

Blinded by Light

I hate driving into the Western sun
Even in decline it jacks across my sight
It's not like the white sheet that falls
When a body part is severed
But with piercing sighted shards
That come aslant like hails of arrows
It blights the vision just as well
Canceling even the peripheral right.

From the left fronts the cause for alarm
The storming giants pushing onward
Sulky King Kongs pawing the air
A shaggy SUV comes barreling down
To my honest Prius intending harm
Such traffic is like the bumper cars
Moved by some befouled lament
Smacking others under the Toyfair tent.

With eyes closed I stew in my lane
At the last they seem to swerve
And regain their rightful place
But the threat is unending, ongoing
An overpass is my needed refuge
That offers some rectifying shade
Some halting recovery of vision
And some sense of what we are made.

It's almost as bad being a pedestrian
Coming out of a shaded building
Meeting the first blast of the Western sun
Stepping through the gates of light
One cannot see where all is bright
Walking is wobbly with dazzled sight.

And that's in an elegant spot!
Try a chewed up parking lot
With broken ridges
Where hay sprouts venture out
All recedes into confusion deplorable
Things are disheveled and deranged
The sidewalks seem to lift at an angle
Only to slope back down again
By habit you look to the left
Fearful of some speeding tyro
Blinded of sight and weak as clay
You could hardly jump to safety
Or insist you had the right of way.
Chopped and fractured macadam
Offers many a slippery fall—
The most feared prospect of all.

Then there's a go at reading
Even if you turn your back
It will poach around your shoulder
Provoke some upsetting glare
Upon the pages that dance to its beat

Line skips and words swallowed
Florid arrangements appear and disappear
On what was once a docile sheet.

How does the declining Western sun
Impose these tribulations
Such troubled flights of imagination?
The noonday sun is brighter far
Yet it casts no such interior fright
It fills the circumambient air
Suffused with accumulated splendor
That reaches heights of "le Roi soleil"
But our sun musters no such display.

Its sightline is tautly strung
Eye-level, singeing, personal, direct
Like squinting through a magnifying glass
The beam is detailed and burns brighter
It can scorch a hole in a piece of paper
It has a particular punishing ire
A more concentrated fire.

The world, through cycles of generations
Does experience its own compensations
The younger rises when the old doth fall
A glum truth familiar to all
So here too age is a differential
Young people don't lament blinding light,
Traffic that cavorts, the ground that rises up

The Western sun is their signal to shine
Coming soon is happy-hour time
Bonanzas allied with the dance of night
They seek no purifying vision
The burning grounds of lustration.
Oedipus blinded by the fury of light.

The Power of Blackness

There is a purity in the schematics of black
It is not like evening dress
Where adornments of brooch or pearl
Can be added to the flitting glow
Black belongs to the dead of the night
It brooks no grace notes, additions
Its devastation is complete.
With no resort to comparisons—
A reliable way for assaying right.

You could be in its middle
And not even know it.
That happens when flying
With instruments inert
There's no scaling up from down
Things get all twisted around
Or being in the depths of the sea
Head and toe as natural props
No longer work to show
Which way is the light.
And that's the point
The properties of black suffer no map
On its own, without address
Ways to travel come only by guess.

Thus it works in the dark above and below

But even at home try negotiating
With the last light out
The passage from desk to bed
The meshed carpeting on the floor
Runs its texture up the walls
Electrical components
From telephone and TV cable
Typewriter and computer snug on a table
All there to draw connections
Might as well be rocks along the shore
The tapping cane cannot scan such
It receives no signal responding to its touch.

Thus we are turned loose again
To discover how long we had strayed
Somewhere we had made a bad turn
But it's not the turn that's wrong
It's the premises that box us in.
In the world of black there is no direction
We are where we know not
Short the distance, the divergence extreme
When caught in the sway of black
In its immediacy supreme.

So Rothko was perhaps right after all
In painting his black without rise or fall
No scenery, no shrubs
For they would be like crumbs
Left for tracking in the dark and the deep

Purity was what he sought
And found it in black
Complete in itself, without aspiration
Annulling all the ways back.

The Crow

Grounded but still brassy
Upstart while all but dazed
Snug fellow of the wanton fly ways
Far from your post
You tumbled into our roost
The hood's warmth taking for a bed
You stood better as a figurehead.

Oh buddy, young crow
You want nothing and give nothing in return
Except your unblinking stare
Corvus, croac, cah cah
Your statuary ware
Has long lost
The feathery gloss
Now like lacquered veneer
In falling shades of black
Like a Rothko painting
Or the panther I cast
In my third-grade art class.

There's much Americana to your wing
Pilgrims clad in uninviting black
Dust bowl survivors
Trying to find their ways back
Whose crease-lined faces

Are filled with sand
Claim you for their own
You are their god of forlorn
Their model in flight and makeshift
They have your staunchest stare
And all the sufficiency that was intended there.

You were perched on Ulysses' right shoulder
When he drew out through the narrows
Out onto the pathless sea
Fought the pull of Brasília's reaches
Just he himself and the circling skies
Such silent facing of the silent deep
Scared Dante halfway out of Hell.
You're not literature's favorite species.
Memorials are not your making.

Your brazen manner suits you right
Your singularity sets you free
Your ship burned and cables cut
The homing instinct is not your style
You feast on garbage dumps
And lighted parking lots
Anyways is how you thrive.

That's all the meaning you afford
Presence to your own accord
Meeting with that which is
You satisfy in the course of flight

You need no anchor to set you right
Embellishments fitting the prince of night
You are the thing itself
The only it it could want
Master of its own surmise.

Coda for the Crow
The bold crow who stumbled into our garage was nurtured back to health in a few days. We placed him in our backyard where he could find seeds and other edibles. Very soon, he was joined by a gaggle of croaking crows and soon disappeared. We would never see him again. But two days later, rummaging through the yard, I came upon a crow's shorn wing. Thus, I concluded, so much for literature, even Huckleberry Finn went out West to be hanged.

But a poem is not undone by matters of fact
It does not require afterwards and aftermaths
Poems have their own fabled content
Their own schedules in time
Their own retinues of retention
Their happenings are fellows of kind
Surprises from the tunnelings of mind.

Poems have their own stories to tell
Their own CV's, recognitions

All responding to their natural fit
A poem marks its own completion
Its own domain—
Where all good things connect.

A poem cannot be a total picture
Four corners of a flawless globe
It does not include all the cases
Even the exceptions that prove the rule
Mere intrusions, conversation's tool
It has what it wants
All its parts in full accord
What the crow meant
Wherever it still stands
Whether or not with wing shorn.

Missing Nothing

Why did they think I could not see
My maiden aunt slipping
A box in brown paper wrap
Between the table and cushioned chair
Like some prestidigitateur
Was it too subtle for me?

And did they think I could not see
My mother nudging my father
For tweaking his trousers
As they sauntered down Front street
On our last Fourth of July?

And did they think I could not hear
My father high on horse back
Boom out to his buddy Yenz
"Would you fuck her?"
Mush-faced pulpy Annie the Fox
Who struck a pose
As she troubled to walk
With me standing so near?

As if I could not absorb
Without stays
That and much, much more
From those gilt-edged long-ago days.

Why even today
Knowing I was fully aware
From her middle row she loosed a pin
That tumbled down her honey-brown hair.

Trackings of the Mind

The pins were scattered by the plunging ball
That sent the boys hopping
To curl their legs along the dash
Above the matted backstop wall.

This was before the alleys went mechanical
When the task of clearing the blasted pins
Sending back the ball again
Was left to nimble young boys
Sweating Sunday nights
School come morning time was tame
Compared with this dodge-ball game.

The muscled men returned from war
Eager to demonstrate their prowess
The balls they pitched were downright wicked
Though somewhat lacking in finesse.

Not all returned from combat
With their minds intact.
Metro clutched the broom
At the Boys' Haven entrance door
Sweeping back and forth
Back and forth like a pendulum clock
The same stretch of the floor.

They called it then "shell-shocked"
We have other names for it now
And more mysterious detections

Well into the night my wife and I sit talking
Up and down both family trees
Including ex-spouses congeries
With vodka and juice in hand
Talking over the events of a life
So many people and places
All come back again
Waiting their turns on call.

That day we had visited
The loveliest woman and most gracious
Her mind reduced to a distorted shell
Seeking to hold by repetition
All that was slipping from her mind
The sweepings of a metronome.

It comes as no surprise
That we should be shunted
To the sidelines of our lives
But we are left dumbfounded
When we outlive our minds.
"J'existe; mais je ne pense pas."

In their world of unknowing
It would be even worse

If they should remember
What they must have been
Or catch some slight glimmer
Of how their wits lie battered
Unaware of when it happened
Who would not reach for the dimmer?

Have mercy on us all,
The little families just starting out
The pin boys wherever scattered
The husky bowlers on a tear
And all those who left the Eastern shores
To hold together in kitchen talk
Hands that will slowly drift apart.

Lost and Found

All the beautiful ladies
Move together as a troupe
Wearing robes of trailing length
Between School and Church
And down the slope
Covered with groves
Under whose stones sisters repose.

Amiable chatter seems to lighten their ways
Questions asked again and over again
Delight so much that no answer need attend
The questions bring laughter enough
Those refurbishments of spring
Politely engendered inquiries
Bring no retention, so they ask again.
Residues of graciousness on the wane.

The responses are like a sudden snow
That covers the cars on city streets
No recognition from these allowed
No disparities of make
No past that exists for the present's sake
Only forms vaguely adhere
That in the density of white appear.

Like when they knew their minds had stalled

Over a name they could not grab and fetch
Even with repeated starts it failed to catch
But was blocked by another name
And saw the alarm on their spouse's face
As if some intruder had violated their place
Or smog blighted the mountains behind
Obliterating lines of bodily kind.
With open arms they happily greet
People they are called to meet
Who vanish in their embraces
Like missing steps down broken stairs.

When they were called to leave
They knew that things were missing
Broken parts that once were theirs.
Belongings they no longer spare
Children's faces grown wan with care.
But they too are figures without names
Tags where all numbers are the same.
With shuffled gait they move
All in shambles
Pitched together they commence a song
"Moon River" reverberates
Mournfully joyously they sing along
"You dream-maker; you heart-breaker"
Down the same sloping deep
Where all the missing parts resort
Their voices gathered to that end
Arranging the soul's last report.

The Sneeze: A Holy Terror

No matter what the outcome
Whether snuffed with tissue
Smothered by hand
Or scattered to the winds
In five traumatic sessions
—once is never dramatic enough—
There is that in a sneeze
That calls for benediction
Or in Arabic, forgiveness
Any prayer bringing surcease
To the rough-house rumbling squeeze.

No such prayer for other emanations
A sneeze is a special concoction
Even when it stutters with false starts
They are just layers mounting up
We know a terrible blast is on its way
That fills with dread
As if the heart were to stop
Requiring a papal injunction
Something read over the dead.

A cough bears no such terror
It crackles like an ice floe breaking up
Or cubes tumbling into a glass
It needs no special interventions

It comes and it goes
No cages are rattled
Or ultra-meanings required.
In fact there is some pleasure
In its spreading throes.

But a sneeze calls for prayer
A fearful swelling act
A meaning issued direct
Like an electric storm
By which the skies are riven
Your name written all over it
Rising like flood waters
Bringing all in its wake
Ascending through the gorge
Where it will explode
Bringing momentary relief
Until another front grabs hold.

But these dread shakings
Are of the body's makings
Their weather belongs to no season.
But are god-given scares
Coming when they will
Without our let or enrollment
Holding court in our body
A genuine element much smaller
Than flood, fire, winds and quakes
But like them endowed by right

With powers and presences
Brooding hints of a primeval fright.

ii.
EPILOGUE: FOR STEVIE

Wandering aloft through inter-net space
With puzzlement in tow
Not detached from nor attached to
Asking with a Yorkshire terrier's face
Backed up, shivering and forlorn
"Where did everyone go?"

RETRIEVALS

1. Atonements

The hero drags a punishing sack
An extremity of grace to atone
Just enough to blunder his step
Or alter his pace to stuttering effect.

Great storage has its own betraying
A club foot, a lump on the back
Those partners in pain
Burdens necessary to assume
Misdirected, distracted, untamed.

That is why he's many years gone
The penalty is actually an urging
A forced uprising that extends the run
A necessary span to permit an unfolding.

> Odysseus doubled his time
> For barking his name
> Dante an equal amount

      For pulling the Pope's tail
      And Shakespeare, mighty Shakespeare
      More sinned against than sinning
      But sinning nonetheless
      How else explain such injured exclaim
      Before relenting he forgave.

But it is not the extent of space
Nor the travel of years that matters
They're only numbers that shadow
The shouldering burden he carries.

Before what he knew as possible only
He now hails home by bone and bearing.
Driven by a strange excess
To arrive at his just intent
Those declarations he intended
Now come unbidden
With nothing else to attend
Fronting the force of the winds
And down the accumulated years

2. Wanderers

You cannot renege on all those years
Though unrequited and of mixed account
They come back in meinie folded
Bearing news from within and without.

Might as well push back the sky
Whose saggings inflect our every view
They are not only that which we know
Their presence informs the ways we go.

Folk of no particular intimacy
Some of scant amiableness
Vulnerabilities must have their day
Like children peddling cookies
Knockings that can't be turned away.

With no force to gather us in
Their cards of varied appeal
Helpless if nobody's home
Or ever will be again.
They stumble to find their places.

>   Vincent, raspy and gruff
>   Enticing with bits of medieval lore
>   Katherine, like her mother,
>   Bent halfway to the floor

John, like Fuzz, a football great
Of more thoughtful merit
Than blackboard teachers can claim
Bob, dwindling down to death,
Breaking only once to regret
Loss of his wife's warm breath.

These are only a few
Not the most notable
Still shadowy and sparse
Whose renewal is plight
By pact I never contrived
Vagrant all these years gone
Faring a wanderer's fate
Departures that never end
Arrivals that never sustain.

Hardly themselves to maintain
They undertake their watchings
Solicitude meant our way
A selflessness so durable
A pathos without stain
Moments of wonder
Like statues in the rain

I'll do my best, I always say
It's not that easy a task
In my hard pallet and darkened hall
I sometimes tarry the call.

These ghostly apparitions
Come not tuckered
Blood to siphon away
Or jostle at the freshing pit
It is myself they come calling about
Keeping me to a just account
These perishable goods I harbor
Are stories heard and markings sounded
Holding me to my stash and say.

Ricardo Quinones is a scholar-critic, professor emeritus of Claremont McKenna College. He is the author of such prize-winning volumes as *The Changes of Cain: Violence and the Lost Brother in Cain-Abel Literature* (1991) and *Dualisms: The Agons of the Modern World* (2007), which was followed by *Erasmus and Voltaire: Why They Still Matter* (2010) and *North/South: The Great European Divide* (2016).

www.ingramcontent.com/pod-product-compliance
Lightning Source LLC
Chambersburg PA
CBHW032053290426
44110CB00012B/1066